DJI RS 4 MINI U

The Complete Step-By-Step Manual

for Beginners and Experts

SAMUEL WOODS

Table of Contents

Chapter 1:
Introduction

Master the Power of Compact Stabilization

Take your filmmaking to the next level with the DJI RS 4 Mini—a lightweight, high-performance gimbal designed for creators who demand smooth, professional-grade footage. Whether you're a beginner or an enthusiast, understanding how to get the most out of your gear is essential.

This user-friendly guide is your essential companion to unlocking the full potential of the RS 4 Mini. Inside, you'll find clear, step-by-step instructions that walk you through setup, balancing, and operation—with zero fluff and zero confusion. Just practical, hands-on advice written for real users like you.

What You'll Learn:

- ❖ Quick and proper setup for any compatible camera
- ❖ Tips to extend battery life and avoid overheating
- ❖ How to master features like ActiveTrack, Panorama, and Timelapse

- ❖ Real-world balancing techniques for consistently smooth shots
- ❖ Easy solutions to common issues—before they ruin your shoot

Whether you're creating content for YouTube, shooting weddings, traveling the world, or crafting cinematic masterpieces, this guide gives you the knowledge and confidence to make the most of every frame.

Simple. Straightforward. Powerful.

The DJI RS 4 MINI USER GUIDE isn't just a manual—it's your creative edge.

Chapter 2:

An Overview of the DJI Rs 4 Mini

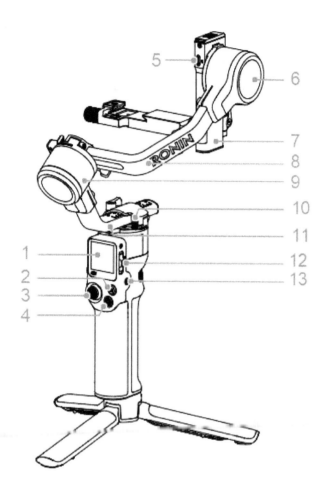

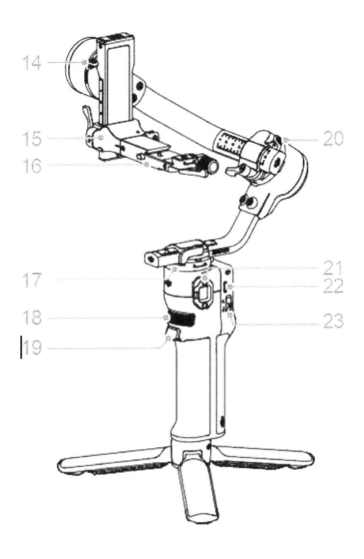

1. Touchscreen

2. M Button

3. Joystick

4. Camera Control Button

5. RSS Camera Control Port (USB-C)

6. Tilt Motor

7. Tilt Axis

8. Roll Axis

9. Roll Motor

10. Pan Lock

11. Pan Axis

12. Gimbal Mode Switch

13. Power Button

14. Tilt Lock

15. Camera Mounting Plate

16. Gimbal Horizontal Plate (Removable Part on the Camera Mounting Plate)

17. Pan Motor

18. Front Dial

19. Trigger

20. Roll Lock

21. NATO Port

22. Charging Port (USB-C)

23. Joystick Mode Switch

MOTORS

QUICK-RELEASE PLATE

BATTERY GRIP

JOYSTICK CONTROLS

Chapter 3:

Utilizing for the First Time

3.1 Attaching the Extended Tripod

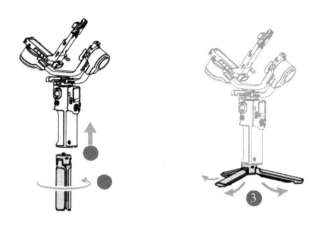

3.2 Charging the Battery

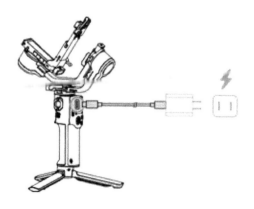

☼ When the device is turned off, press the power button to see the battery level on the screen.

3.3 Mounting the Camera

Supported Lenses and Camera

Verify that the total weight of the camera, lens, and additional accessories does not exceed the load limit by visiting https://www.dji.com/rs-4-mini/specs. For a list of compatible camera lenses and control functions, see the Ronin Series Compatibility List.

Getting ready

1. Take off the lens cap and make sure the memory card and batteries are in the camera.

2. Ensure that the gimbal is turned off.

3. Adjust both axes as shown in the image below, move the tilt and roll locks to the unlocked position, and then lock the axes.

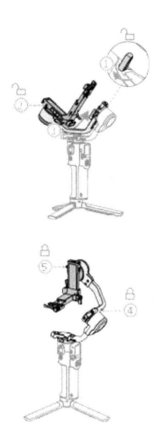

The Upper Quick-Release Plate Attachment

Using the 1/4" screw included in the screw kit, fasten the top quick-release plate to the camera's bottom. Before tightening the screw, snap the movable positioning guide onto the camera body.

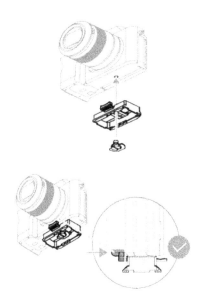

Shooting Horizontally

1. Engage the horizontal plate by moving the lever to the unlocked position ①, then move it to the locked position ③ after inserting the bottom quick-release plate ②.

2. After the top quick-release plate has been inserted, move the lever to the locked position ⑥. Then, move the lever on the lower quick-release plate to the unlocked position ④.

11

❖ Press the safety lock next to the lever while moving the
lever to the unlocked position to remove the camera
from the bottom quick-release plate.

❖ To remove the bottom quick-release plate, push the horizontal plate's safety lock while moving the horizontal plate's lever to the unlocked position.

Shooting Vertically

1. To remove the horizontal plate ③, loosen ① and push the knob ②. Next, attach the plate on the gimbal vertically ④ and tighten the knob ⑤.

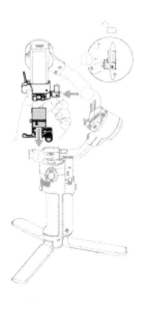

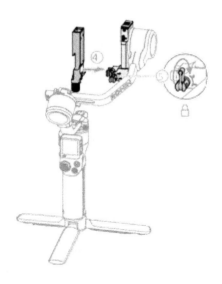

2. Adjust the horizontal plate's lever to the unlocked position ①, then insert the lower quick-release plate ② and, once engaged, adjust the lever to the locked position ③.

3. After the top quick-release plate has been inserted, move the lever to the locked position ⑥. Then, move the lever on the lower quick-release plate to the unlocked position ④.

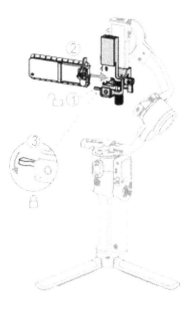

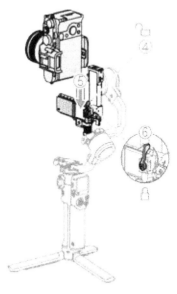

15

3.4 Balancing

Before utilizing the gimbal, make sure that the roll, pan, tilt, and vertical tilt are all balanced in accordance with the shooting requirements. This guarantees the gimbal's full functioning and the steadiness of videos.

⚠ An uneven gimbal may shorten battery life and impact video steadiness.

The gadget may overheat and enter hibernation if there is a significant imbalance.

Prior to Balancing

1. Turn on the camera if you're using an optical zoom lens and choose the focal length if you're using a varifocal lens before balancing.
2. Prior to balancing, make sure the DJI RS 4 Mini is turned off or in sleep mode.

Steps for Balancing

To see the instructional video, click the link or scan the QR code.

https://s.dji.com/guide85

3.4 Activation

The DJI RS 4 Mini must be activated using the Ronin app. To activate your gadget, do the actions listed below:

1. Turn on your smartphone by pressing and holding the power button, then use the touchscreen to choose your preferred language.
2. To download the Ronin app, scan the QR code on the touchscreen.
3. Turn on Bluetooth on your phone. Open the Ronin app, then sign in using your DJI credentials. Choose the device, enter the 12345678-default password, then follow the instructions to activate the gimbal. Activation requires an internet connection.

It may be used up to five times without turning on the gimbal. Activation is then necessary in order to continue using it.

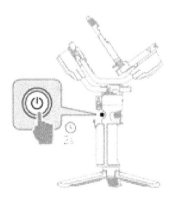

Visit https://www.dji.com/mobile/downloads/djiapp/dji-ronin or scan the QR code below if the Ronin app cannot be downloaded after scanning the code on the device's screen.

3.5. Firmware Update

The Ronin app will alert users once fresh firmware becomes available. Follow the on-screen directions to update the firmware. During the firmware upgrade, DO NOT turn off the gimbal or close the application. Try again after restarting the Ronin app and gimbal if the update doesn't work.

❖ During upgrading, make sure the mobile device is online and the gimbal has enough power.

❖ During the update process, it is typical for the gimbal to automatically unlock, lock, and reboot.

3.6. Connecting a Camera

The DJI RS 4 Mini may be connected to the camera via a camera control wire or Bluetooth. To see the instructional video, click the link or scan the QR code.

This is the video: https://www.dji.com/rs-4-mini

3.7. Auto Tune

To begin the automated calibration process, press and hold the M button and trigger.

⚠ The gimbal should be placed on a level, stable platform. When the gimbal is automatically calibrated, DO NOT move it. During the calibration, it is common for the gimbal to shake or produce noises.

Chapter 4:

Operations

4.1. Button and Port Functions

Buttons

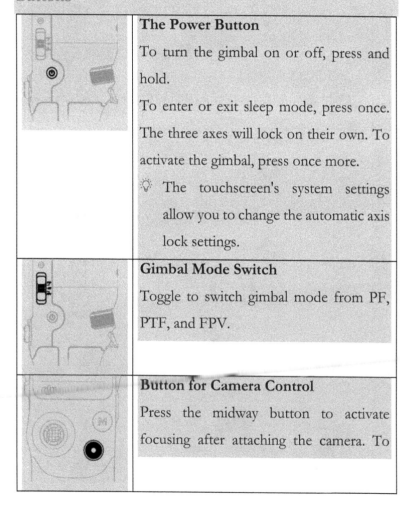

	The Power Button To turn the gimbal on or off, press and hold. To enter or exit sleep mode, press once. The three axes will lock on their own. To activate the gimbal, press once more. ☼ The touchscreen's system settings allow you to change the automatic axis lock settings.
	Gimbal Mode Switch Toggle to switch gimbal mode from PF, PTF, and FPV.
	Button for Camera Control Press the midway button to activate focusing after attaching the camera. To

	begin or stop recording, press once. To snap a picture, press and hold. ☀ For comprehensive details on compatible cameras, see the Ronin Series Compatibility List.
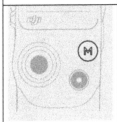	**The M Button** To automatically capture pictures, press once. On the touchscreen, the button's function may be changed to C1/Fn1 Button Mapping. To enter Sport Mode, press and hold. The gimbal's follow speed significantly rises in Sport Mode. It works well for taking pictures of subjects that move quickly and unexpectedly. Holding down the M button, push the trigger twice: Go into Sport Mode and stay there. To leave, repeat.
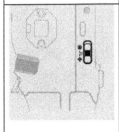	**Joystick Mode Switch** Press down to switch to gimbal movement control on the joystick. Push up: Select zoom control from the joystick mode.

Joystick

In order to control the gimbal's movement, move the joystick up and down to adjust its tilt, and move it left and right to adjust its pan.

The zoom may be controlled by moving the joystick up and down.

Turn on Sony cameras' power zoom so that the joystick can operate the camera's power zoom.

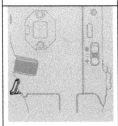

Trigger

To enter Lock mode, press and hold. The gimbal will not react to grip movement while in lock mode. Press and hold the trigger to enter FPV mode when it has been set up on the touchscreen.

To re-center the gimbal, press twice.

To rotate the gimbal 180 degrees so that the camera is facing you (selfie mode), press three times,

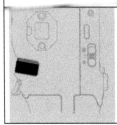

The front dial

By default, turn controls the focus. The touchscreen allows you to adjust the settings. For more information, see the Touchscreen section.

☼ For comprehensive details on features that are supported, see the Ronin Series Compatibility List.

Ports

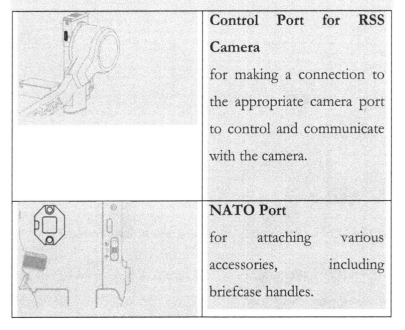

	Control Port for RSS Camera for making a connection to the appropriate camera port to control and communicate with the camera.
	NATO Port for attaching various accessories, including briefcase handles.

Home

You may choose the gimbal follow mode , follow speed/sensitivity, check the balancing state 🖸, and conduct auto calibration ↳ on this interface. The battery level and gimbal connection status are shown in the status bar at the top of the touchscreen.

To keep everything balanced, **Auto-Tune** modifies the gimbal's rigidity.

Various colors are used to represent the **balance status**.

To set slow, medium, fast, or custom follow speeds, tap the Follow Speed/Sensitivity icon. There are also many sensitivity modes available. The Smooth mode is inherited by the Adhere to the Ronin series stabilizers' sensitivity to guarantee seamless start and stop motions and organic transitions in your video.

When in responsive mode, the gimbal reacts to hand motions during start and stop faster, making the experience more responsive.

⋄❖ It is advised to carry out automatic calibration if, after gimbal balancing, the balance status symbol becomes red when the focal length, lens, or camera are changed, or if the gimbal rattles uncontrollably.

❖ If the gimbal is not stable enough, it is advised to raise the motor strength; if it begins to wobble, it is advised to decrease the stiffness.

Slide Down - Control Center

This interface allows you to do things like change the quiet mode ◀», connect to Bluetooth ✱», and lock screen settings ▣.

You may do parameter restoration, auto lock settings, and gimbal auto check under the System Settings menu. The following functionalities are also accessible.

- ❖ **Disable Selfie:** This stops recording from being interrupted when you inadvertently enter selfie mode.
- ❖ **Orbit Follow:** This feature allows the gimbal to move more smoothly while taking arc shots.
- ❖ **Push Mode:** Allows tilt and pan axis control by hand.
- ❖ **Horizontal Calibration:** If the gimbal is uneven or the axis is drifting, attempt horizontal calibration or manual calibration.
- ❖ **Auto down:** After ten minutes of being locked and not in use, the gimbal will shut down on its own.

Slide Up - Gimbal Settings

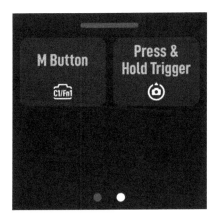

You may choose the functions for holding the trigger, hitting the
M button, and turning the dial on this interface, as well as change
the speed and smoothness of the joystick.

❖ The lower the smoothness setting, the more sensitive the
movement of the gimbal.

❖ Map the C1/Fn1 button function of the camera.

1. Map the M button to the C1 button on Sony cameras
(A7S3, A7M3, ZV-1) or the Fn1 button on Nikon
cameras (Z50, Z6II).

2. Complete the settings on the camera for the C1/Fn1
button. It can only be used when paired with a
camera using Bluetooth.

No Signal Input will appear on the screen if there isn't an intelligent tracking module attached. When the intelligent tracking module is attached, composition, ActiveTrack Speed, and gestures may be adjusted on this page.

Composition: When composition is modified to center tracking topic, the topic monitored will be relocated to the center of the ActiveTrack display.

The gimbal will preserve the current composition while ActiveTrack is enabled with Keep Current Framing.

ActiveTrack Speed: For live broadcasting, slow speed offers smooth tracking. Fast speed is ideal for high-motion scenarios or close-up circular views, while medium speed is good for parallel tracking.

✓ The ActiveTrack view is not visible on the touchscreen.
✓ Because of changes in the camera, lens, and shooting distance, the subject in Center Tracking Subject may not always remain precisely centered. Use the joystick to change the composition if this occurs.

4.3 Gimbal Follow Modes

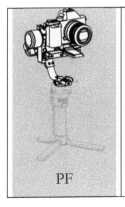 PF	PF: Pan follow, in which the grip's movement is followed only by the pan axis. Ideal for situations like going from left to right or shooting emerging walk-through and arc shots

PFF	PTF: Pan and tilt follow, in which the grip's movement is followed by the tilt and pan axes. Ideal for situations involving slanting motion.
FPV	FPV: Pan, tilt, and roll follow, in which the grip's movement is followed by all three axes. Ideal for situations when the camera is rotating.
Custom	**Custom:** As needed, turns on or off any axis follow. Disabling the three axes activates lock mode. In lock mode, none of the three axes will follow the grip's movement. Ideal for fast response shots and fluid tracking shots.
3D Roll 360	When the tilt axis is 90° upward and the camera lens is vertically upward in 3D Roll

	360 mode, you may use the joystick to control the pan axis' 360° rotation. Ideal for pictures that rotate.

4.4   Gimbal Operation Modes

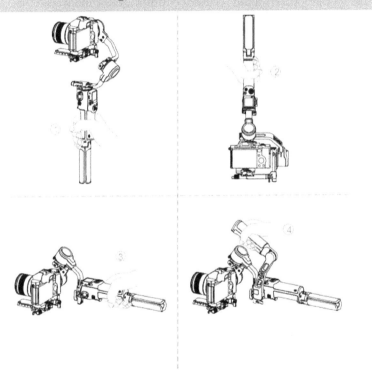

1. **The Upright Mode** is the gimbal's default operating mode, and it works well for the majority of shooting situations, including running and walking shots.

2. **The Underslung Mode:** The camera is positioned lower, and the gimbal is inverted. This setting works well for tracking things on the ground and other low-angle photography.

3. **The Flashlight Mode:** Like a flashlight, the gimbal is held horizontally. You may photograph in limited places using this setting.

4. **The Briefcase Mode:** This mode, which makes low-angle camera movements more natural, requires the briefcase handle to be attached. The knob allows you to change the briefcase handle's angle. The gimbal's 1/4"-20 mounting holes and cold shoes enable the attachment of external monitors to aid in shooting.

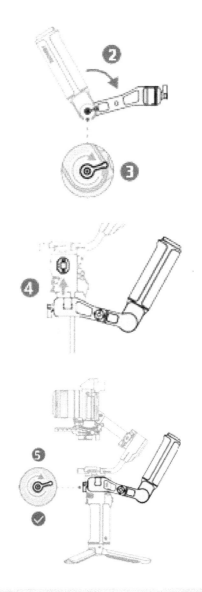

4.5   Ronin App Settings

The Ronin app allows users to change motor parameters, user settings, and joystick choices, as well as to activate the gimbal, update the firmware, and access intelligent capabilities. You may also access training videos, the user manual, and system status.

4.6 Intelligent Tracking Module

Overview

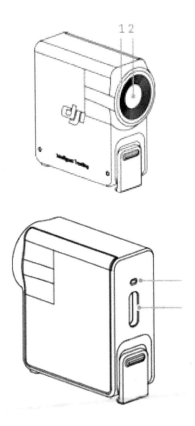

1. Ring light

Battery Level

Solid Red ActiveTrack disabled(in sleep mode) or sub- ject lost.

Solid Green ActiveTrack in use

Blinks Green Subject lost temporarily

Solid Yellow Composition being adjusted

Blinks Yellow Countdown for taking a picture or recording (shutter triggered after 3s of blinking)

2. Tracking Lens
3. Status Indicator
Light signals and meanings are consistent with the ring light.
4. USB-C Data Port

To upgrade the firmware, connect to a computer.

Installation

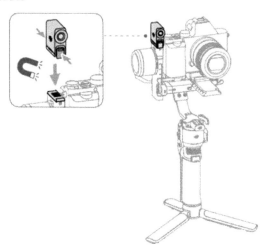

Slide right from the home page to access the ActiveTrack settings panel after installing the intelligent tracking module, then make the necessary adjustments based on your shooting requirements. See Slide Right—ActiveTrack Settings for specific instructions.

✓ Verify that the magnetic attachment is in place if, after installation, the status indication does not illuminate.

✓ The tracking module automatically switches to sleep mode and shuts off the indication if it is inactive for more than five minutes. Press the gimbal's trigger to activate the module.

Tracking and Shooting

- ✓ Using it in low light or backlight conditions is not advised.

- ✓ Maintain a distance of 0.5 to 10 meters between the subject and the tracking lens when tracking.

Using a joystick and buttons for control

To activate or deactivate the ActiveTrack, press the trigger.

After tracking the subject, you may modify the composition using the joystick.

To recenter the gimbal and turn off ActiveTrack, press the trigger twice.

The gimbal mode switch allows you to switch between ActiveTrack modes while shooting.

Only the pan axis may follow in Pan Follow (PF) mode; in Pan and Tilt Follow (PTF) mode, both tilt and pan axes may follow; ActiveTrack is not supported in Full Follow (FPV) mode.

The gimbal handle should point toward the subject being tracked when using a mid-low camera position.

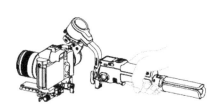

Control via Gesture

Turn on tracking: either push the trigger or make the motion to the camera. The indication becomes completely green.

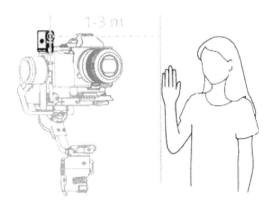

People near the lens and in the center of the vision are given priority by the tracking module, which only allows following. One to three meters should separate the tracked subject from the tracking lens.

Composition modification: During tracking, make any necessary compositional adjustments. Make the gesture visible to the camera. Tracking is immediately halted when the signal goes solid yellow. It is possible to move the topic to the desired location inside the frame.

To verify the composition, repeat the motion. Tracking immediately restarts when the signal becomes solid green.

Put an end to tracking: either make the motion or pull the trigger once again. The indication becomes completely red.

Shooting: You may use it to begin a countdown for shooting a picture or to start and stop recording, whether or not tracking is enabled. As the countdown progresses, the indicator flashes yellow.

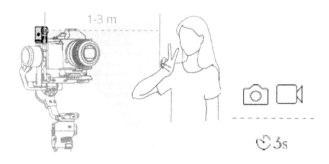

Update the Firmware

To update the firmware, the tracking module must be linked to a computer.

1. Go to https://www.dji.com/rs-4-mini/downloads and get the firmware package that is needed.

2. Attach the tracking module to the PC using the USB-C connection that comes with it.

3. Put the firmware package (a file with a .bin extension) that you obtained into the tracking module's root directory.

4. Cut off the USB connection after copying.

5. Reattach the computer and tracking module. The update procedure will be initiated automatically by the tracking module. The status indicator will alternate between blinking green and red. Throughout the procedure, DO NOT cut the connection.

6. The update is complete when the status indication stays solid red.

Chapter 5:
Grip/Built-In Battery

For information about the gimbal battery and gimbal running time, refer to https:// www.dji.com/rs-4-mini/specs

5.1   Safety Guidelines

Before using this device, familiarize yourself with its features by reading the user handbook. Improper use of the product may lead to severe injury, damage to the product, and damage to personal property. This product is very advanced. It involves some basic mechanical skills and must be used carefully and sensibly. Injury or damage to the product or other property might arise from not using this product in a safe and responsible way.

Children should not use this product without close adult supervision. DO NOT make any changes to this product beyond what SZ DJI TECHNOLOGY CO., LTD. has supplied in the documentation. Instructions for operation, maintenance, and safety are included in these safety guidelines. To operate the device properly and prevent damage or severe harm, it is essential that you read and heed all of the directions and cautions in the user manual before assembling, setting up, or using it.

Use of Grip

1. AVOID letting the grip come into touch with fluids of any type. The grip should never be left outside in the rain or next to a moisture source. AVOID letting the grasp fall into the

water. Chemical breakdown may take place if the battery's inside water, which might cause the battery to catch fire or even explode.

2. Place the grip in a secure, open location right away if it accidentally falls into the water. Until the grip is totally dry, keep a safe distance from it. Please follow the instructions in the Grip Disposal section to properly dispose of the grip, and do not use it again.

3. Use a dry powder fire extinguisher, water, sand, or a fire blanket to put out any flames.

4. A bloated, leaking, or damaged grip should not be used or charged. For more help, get in touch with DJI or an authorized DJI dealer if the grip seems strange.

5. The ideal temperature range for the grip is -10° to 45° C (-14° to 113° F). Using the grip at temperatures higher than 50° C (122° F) may result in an explosion or fire. Using a grip below 0° C (32° F) may cut down on operating time considerably.

6. AVOID using the battery close to high-voltage transmission lines or in areas with intense electromagnetic or electrostatic fields.

7. To prevent the battery from leaking, igniting, or exploding, DO NOT dismantle or puncture the grip in any manner.

8. Batteries should not be dropped or struck. Heavy things should not be placed on the grip.

9. The battery's electrolytes are very corrosive. See a doctor right away if any electrolytes get in your eyes or on your skin. Wash the affected area with fresh running water for at least 15 minutes.

10. If dropped, DO NOT utilize the grip.

11. Batteries should not be heated. The grip should not be placed in a pressurized container or in a microwave oven.

12. AVOID physically cutting the grip.

13. Use a fresh, dry towel to wipe the grip terminals.

☼ Before using, confirm that the grip is completely charged.

☼ Charge the grip right away if a low-battery alert occurs.

Getting charged

1. When charging, DO NOT leave the grip unattended. Charge the grip away from combustible objects and away from combustible surfaces like wood or carpet.

2. Leakage, overheating, or battery damage may result if charging the grip outside of the 5° to 40° C (41° to 104° F) temperature range. The optimal temperature range for charging is 22° to 28° C (72° to 82° F).

☼ When the grip is full, it is intended to cease charging. However, it is advisable to keep an eye on the charging process and release the grip after the battery is completely charged.

Storage

1. Keep the batteries out of children's and animals' reach.
2. Charge the grip till the battery level reaches between 30% and 50% if it will be kept in storage for a long time.
3. A furnace or heater is an example of a heat source where the grasp should not be left. On hot days, DO NOT leave the grip inside a car. The recommended temperature range for storage is 22° to 28° C (72° to 82° F).
4. Maintain a dry grip.

☼ If the grip won't be utilized for ten days or more, release it to 40% to 65%. may significantly increase battery life.

☼ The grip will go to sleep mode if it is kept in storage for a long time and the battery runs out. To get out of sleep state, recharge the grip.

☼ The grip will go to sleep mode if it is kept in storage for a long time and the battery runs out. To get out of sleep state, recharge the grip.

Maintenance

⚠ 1. When the temperature is too hot or too low, DO NOT use the grip.

⚠ 2. The battery should not be kept at temperatures lower than 0° C (32° F) or hotter than 45° C (113° F).

☼ Extended periods of inactivity may shorten battery life.

☼ To maintain the grip in excellent shape, fully charge and discharge it once every three months.

Notice of Travel

1. The grip must be depleted until the battery level is less than 30% before being carried on an airline trip. Store the grip in a vented area and only release it in a fireproof area.

2. Avoid holding onto metal items, including jewelry, watches, hairpins, and spectacles.3. A damaged grip or one with a battery level over 30% should not be transported.Elimination Only after a full discharge should you dispose of the grip in designated recycling boxes. The grip should not be put in ordinary garbage cans. Adhere strictly to your local laws governing battery recycling and disposal. 1. For further help, get in touch with a qualified battery disposal or recycling company if the grip is deactivated and the battery cannot be completely depleted.

2. If the grip cannot be turned on after over-dispelling, dispose of it right away.

Chapter 6:

Appendix

6.1   Maintenance

There is no waterproofing on the gimbal. When using it, be cautious to shield it from water and dust. It is advised you use a gentle, dry towel to clean the gimbal after usage. Cleaning solutions should not be sprayed on the gimbal.

6.2 Specification

Specs

Peripheral

Accessory Port	NATO Port 1/4"-20 Mounting Hole RSS Camera Control Port (USB-C) Pogo Pin (compatible with the DJI RS Intelligent Tracking Module)
Battery	Model: BHX724-3100-7.2 Type: LiPo 2S Capacity: 3100 mAh Energy: 22.32 Wh Max Runtime: 13 hours (stationary) * Charging Specification: 9 V/2.5 A Charging Time: Approx. 1 hour and 50 minutes ** Suggested Charging Temperature: 5° to 40° C (41° to 104° F)

* Measured with the equipment in a level and stationary state and the gimbal balanced. When the gimbal is in motion, the operating time will be reduced.
** Tested in a 25° C (77° F) environment while using a 30W charger.

Connections	Bluetooth 5.1 USB-C Charging Port
Ronin App Requirements	iOS 14.0 or above Android 9.0 or above
Languages Supported by the Touchscreen	English, Simplified Chinese, Traditional Chinese, German, French, Korean, Japanese, Spanish, Portuguese (Brazil), Russian, Thai

Working Performance

Tested Payload	0.4-2 kg (0.88-4.4 lbs)
Maximum Controlled Rotation Speed	Pan: 360°/s Tilt: 360°/s Roll: 360°/s
Mechanical Range	Pan Axis: 360° continuous rotation Roll Axis: -95° to +235° Tilt Axis: -110° to +210°
Axis Locks	Auto
Vertical Shooting	Supported

Mechanical & Electrical Properties

Operating Frequency	2.4000-2.4835 GHz
Bluetooth Transmitter Power	< 4 dBm

Operating Temperature	-10° to 45° C (14° to 113° F)
Weight	Gimbal: Approx. 890 g (2 lbs) (including the Quick-Release Plate and excluding the tripod) Extended Grip/Tripod: Approx. 140 g (0.3 lbs)
Dimensions	Folded: 236×64×316 mm (L×W×H, excluding the tripod and the Quick-Release Plate) Unfolded: 175×182×338 mm (L×W×H, excluding camera, tripod, and the Quick-Release Plate)

Accessories

DJI RS Intelligent Tracking Module	Weight: 19 g Dimensions: 33.5×17.5×38.5 mm (L×W×H) Tracking Distance: 0.5-10 m Operating Environment: Illuminance > 20 lux Trigger Modes: Gimbal trigger, gesture Gesture Functions: Start/stop of tracking, start/stop of recording, framing adjustment Power Consumption: < 1 W Operation Temperature: -10 to 45° C (14° to 113° F) Mounting Method: Magnetic attachment
DJI RS 4 Mini Phone Holder	Weight: 92.5 g Dimensions: 50×48×95.15 mm (L×W×H)

Chapter 7:

Conclusion

The DJI RS 4 Mini isn't just a piece of gear—it's your gateway to smooth, cinematic footage in a compact, user-friendly form. Whether you're a beginner exploring filmmaking or an experienced creator on the move, this gimbal gives you the power to capture your vision with clarity and control.

In this guide, you've learned how to:

> ➢ Set up and balance your gimbal with ease
> ➢ Master essential modes like ActiveTrack and Timelapse
> ➢ Solve common issues quickly and confidently
> ➢ Maximize performance for different shooting scenarios

Now that you're equipped with the knowledge, the rest is up to you. The more you use your RS 4 Mini, the more intuitive and powerful it becomes. Push boundaries, explore new techniques, and most importantly—keep creating.

7.1 Final Tip:

Stay connected with DJI's official updates and the community of users for new features, compatibility lists, and creative inspiration.

Thank you for trusting this guide to be part of your creative journey. May every frame you shoot be smoother, sharper, and more inspiring than the last.

Film with purpose. Stabilize with precision. Create without limits.

www.ingramcontent.com/pod-product-compliance
Lightning Source LLC
Chambersburg PA
CBHW061038050326

40689CB00012B/2887